WITHDRAWN

## National Landmarks

# The Statue of Liberty

by Kathleen W. Deady

**Consultant:**
Paul R. Baker
Professor Emeritus of History
New York University

# Bridgestone Books
an imprint of Capstone Press
Mankato, Minnesota

Bridgestone Books are published by Capstone Press
151 Good Counsel Drive, P.O. Box 669, Mankato, Minnesota 56002
http://www.capstone-press.com

*Library of Congress Cataloging-in-Publication Data*
Deady, Kathleen W.
    The Statue of Liberty/by Kathleen W. Deady.
    p. cm.—(National landmarks)
    Includes bibliographical references and index.
    ISBN 0-7368-1115-X
    Summary: Discusses the history of the Statue of Liberty, its designer, construction of
the memorial, its location, and its importance to the people of the United States.
    1. Statue of Liberty (New York, N.Y.)—Juvenile literature. 2. Statue of Liberty (New York,
N.Y.)—History—Juvenile literature. 3. New York (N.Y.)—Buildings, structures, etc.—Juvenile
literature. [1. Statue of Liberty (New York, N.Y.) 2. National monuments. 3. Statues.] I. Title.
II. Series.
F128.64.L6 D425 2002
974.7'1—dc21                                            2001003303

**Editorial Credits**

Erika Mikkelson, editor; Karen Risch, product planning editor; Linda Clavel, cover designer
    and interior layout designer; Erin Scott, SARIN Creative, illustrator; Alta Schaffer,
    photo researcher

**Photo Credits**

Archive Photos, 8, 12, 14
Digital Stock, cover, 1, 6
Museum of the City of New York/Archive Photos, 10
North Wind Picture Archives, 16
Visuals Unlimited/M. Long, 4; C.P. George, 18; Bill Banaszewski, 20

1 2 3 4 5 6 07 06 05 04 03 02

# Table of Contents

# Fast Facts

★ **Formal Name:** Liberty Enlightening the World

★ **Nicknames:** Lady Liberty, Liberty, Mother of Exiles, Colossus

★ **Construction Materials:** The outside of the statue is made of copper. The copper is 3/32 of an inch (2.38 millimeters) thick. The inside of the statue is a steel framework. The statue bends slightly when the wind blows.

★ **Height:** The statue is 305 feet, 1 inch (93 meters) from the ground to the tip of the torch. The statue itself is 151 feet, 1 inch (46.05 meters) tall. The pedestal rises 154 feet (46.94 meters).

★ **Weight:** The copper in the statue weighs 62,000 pounds (28,123 kilograms). The steel in the statue's frame weighs about 250,000 pounds (113,400 kilograms).

★ **The Crown:** The crown has 25 windows in it. They stand for 25 gemstones found on Earth. The crown's seven spikes represent the seven oceans and seven continents of the world. Visitors climb 354 steps up to the crown.

★ **Date Built:** Édouard de Laboulaye thought of the idea for the statue in 1865. It was completed and dedicated in 1886.

★ **Cost:** The statue cost about $600,000 in the 1880s. The pedestal cost about $270,000. The restoration in the 1980s cost about $31 million.

★ **Visitors:** More than 2 million people visit the Statue of Liberty each year.

NEW YORK

New Hampshire

Vermont

Massachusetts

Rhode Island

Connecticut

Pennsylvania

New Jersey

Statue of Liberty

Atlantic Ocean

New Jersey

Hudson River

New York

Liberty State Park

Ellis Island

Statue of Liberty

New York Harbor

# The Statue of Liberty

The Statue of Liberty was a gift of friendship from France to the people of the United States. The statue is a symbol of freedom and hope for people around the world.

The Statue of Liberty is a woman standing on a pedestal. She wears a long flowing robe and a spiked crown. Her left hand holds a tablet with the date July 4, 1776. The United States declared its independence from Great Britain on this date. Her right hand holds a torch high in the air. The torch represents liberty.

The Statue of Liberty National Monument stands on Liberty Island in New York Harbor. Nearby Ellis Island also is part of the national monument. Ellis Island once was an immigration station. During the 1800s, millions of people left their countries and came to America. These immigrants entered through Ellis Island. Today, Ellis Island is a museum.

**The Statue of Liberty stands on Liberty Island in New York Harbor.**

# History of the Idea

On July 4, 1776, the 13 American colonies declared independence from Great Britain. The colonies wanted to form a new country. But Great Britain did not want to lose the 13 colonies.

The colonies fought the Revolutionary War (1775–1783) against Great Britain. France supported the colonies in their battle. The colonies won the war and formed the United States. France and the United States became friends.

In 1865, Frenchman Édouard de Laboulaye had an idea. He thought France should give a statue to the United States. This gift would celebrate the countries' friendship. It also would celebrate the United States' freedom.

A French sculptor named Frédéric-Auguste Bartholdi liked the idea. He started planning the statue. In 1871, Bartholdi traveled to the United States. He looked for a site for the statue. He chose Bedloe's Island in New York Harbor.

**French historian Édouard de Laboulaye was a leader in France's fight to end slavery.**

# Designing the Statue of Liberty

Bartholdi was excited about designing the statue. He had seen the great monuments that ancient Egyptians built. He wanted his statue to be huge.

Bartholdi designed a hollow statue that would be 151 feet (46 meters) tall. He chose copper for the outside. This metal is easy to bend and mold. The copper would wrap like skin around the statue's frame.

Building the frame was difficult. Bartholdi needed help. French engineer Alexandre-Gustave Eiffel designed the frame. It had an iron tower in the middle. Strong iron bars would connect the copper to the tower.

From 1882 to 1884, American architect Richard Morris Hunt designed the pedestal to support the statue. It would raise the statue more than 150 feet (46 meters) in the air. Hunt used concrete for the foundation, or base, of the pedestal. Large granite blocks make up the pedestal.

**Frédéric-Auguste Bartholdi designed the Statue of Liberty.**

France and the United States worked together on the project. In 1875, Laboulaye formed the French-American Union. This group ran the project and raised money to build the statue. The French fund-raising went well. The French people raised $400,000. Work on the statue began.

In 1876, people in the United States formed the American Committee. This committee would raise funds to build the pedestal. But Americans were not very interested. U.S. fund-raising started slowly.

By 1884, the French had finished the statue. But the American Committee had run out of money. Work had stopped on the pedestal.

Finally, publisher Joseph Pulitzer helped. He wrote stories in his New York newspaper. He told people of the statue's importance. He asked people to give money to finish the pedestal. He promised to publish their names in his newspaper. Finally, people gave money so workers could finish the pedestal.

**Publisher Joseph Pulitzer helped raise money for the Statue of Liberty's pedestal.**

# Building the Statue of Liberty

Bartholdi began building the statue in Paris in 1875. Many sculptors, carpenters, plasterers, and metalworkers helped him.

First, workers built wooden models. They covered the models with plaster to make a mold of the basic shape. Next, workers built wooden frames in the shape of the plaster mold. They placed copper sheets on the molds. They then hammered the copper sheets. The hammering formed the copper into the shape of the plaster.

In 1880, Eiffel designed the frame to hold the copper skin. Workers built the frame outside of the Paris workshop. They attached the molded copper sheets to the frame. Everything fit together like a giant puzzle.

In 1884, workers finished the statue. Workers then took it apart. They packed it into 214 crates and shipped it to New York. The pedestal was finished in April 1886. Workers put the statue back together on the pedestal. The Statue of Liberty was in place on October 25, 1886.

**Workers built the wooden frames for the Statue of Liberty inside Bartholdi's shop.**

# The Statue of Liberty Completed

Laboulaye and Bartholdi had wanted to build the statue for America's 100th anniversary in 1876. But many delays prevented the statue's completion. Bartholdi did finish the right arm and torch. They were displayed in Philadelphia in 1876.

The dedication ceremony was held on October 28, 1886. New York City officially named this date Bartholdi Day. President Grover Cleveland accepted the Statue of Liberty for the United States.

Ferdinand-Marie de Lesseps spoke for Laboulaye. Lesseps led the French-American Union after Laboulaye died in 1884. William M. Evarts, a New York senator, spoke next. Evarts organized the fund-raising in America.

Many people boarded boats and sailed into the harbor to see the statue. A parade of 20,000 people marched downtown to the harbor. Later, people shot fireworks that lit up the night sky over Lady Liberty.

**On October 28, 1886, people celebrated the dedication of the Statue of Liberty.**

# Changes to the Statue of Liberty

Over the years, changes have been made to the Statue of Liberty. It originally had a wooden staircase inside. Workers replaced it with a larger iron spiral staircase. Tourists then could climb up to the crown. In 1907, workers put an elevator in the pedestal.

Workers also replaced the torch. The original flame was solid copper. In 1916, sculptor Gutzon Borglum cut large windows in the copper. Workers placed lamps in the windows to light up the flame at night.

In 1982, workers completely restored the statue. They strengthened the right arm and replaced the torch. The new flame is painted gold to reflect sunlight. Workers replaced many rusty beams in the frame. They painted the statue's inside and cleaned its outside.

President Ronald Reagan rededicated the Statue of Liberty in 1986. Americans celebrated the statue's first 100 years.

**Sculptor Gutzon Borglum cut windows into the torch in 1916. Workers replaced this torch in 1982.**

# Visiting the Statue of Liberty

More than 2 million people visit the Statue of Liberty National Monument each year. Groups of schoolchildren travel there on field trips. Visitors take a ferry across New York Harbor to Liberty Island. Some people climb the steps or ride the elevator to the top of the pedestal. Other visitors climb higher up the spiral staircase. They can look out from the windows in the crown.

People also visit the museum in the pedestal. They see the original flame on display. One exhibit shows how workers built the statue.

Today, Ellis Island also is a museum. Exhibits explain how immigrants came to America. Videos and photographs tell the story of early immigrants.

The Statue of Liberty is the world's tallest statue. The Statue of Liberty continues to be an important symbol of freedom and hope to the world.

**The Statue of Liberty is a famous U.S. landmark. People from around the world visit the statue.**

# Important Dates

★ 1865—Laboulaye has the idea to give the statue to the United States.

★ 1871—Bartholdi comes to the United States to get support for the idea and look for a site.

★ 1875—People from the French-American Union raise money for the statue. Workers begin building the statue.

★ 1876—Workers finish the right arm and torch. They ship them to Philadelphia for a display that celebrates America's first 100 years. People in the United States form the American Committee to raise money for the pedestal.

★ 1880—Eiffel designs the frame for the statue.

★ 1882–1884—Hunt designs the pedestal for the statue.

★ 1884—Workers finish building the statue in Paris.

Joseph Pulitzer helps to raise money for the pedestal.

★ 1885—Workers take apart the statue and ship it to New York.

★ 1886—Workers in New York finish the pedestal in April.

Workers put the statue back together on top of the pedestal. They finish on October 25. President Grover Cleveland dedicates the statue on October 28.

★ 1924—The Statue of Liberty becomes a national monument.

★ 1965—Ellis Island becomes part of the Statue of Liberty National Monument.

★ 1986—Workers finish a complete restoration of the statue.

President Ronald Reagan rededicates the statue.

# Words to Know

**architect** (AR-ki-tekt)—a person who designs buildings
**colony** (KAWL-uh-nee)—a settlement in a distant land that is ruled by another country
**dedicate** (DED-uh-kayt)—to open officially for the public to use
**exhibit** (eg-ZIB-it)—a display that shows something to the public
**frame** (FRAYM)—a structure that shapes and supports something
**immigrant** (IM-uh-gruhnt)—a person who leaves one country to live in another country
**pedestal** (PED-es-tuhl)—the bottom support of a statue or pillar
**plaster** (PLAS-tur)—a mixture of lime, sand, and water that dries hard
**sculptor** (SKUHLP-tur)—an artist who carves statues out of stone or wood
**spiral** (SPEYE-ruhl)—a circle that goes up or down around a center point
**symbol** (SIM-buhl)—an object that stands for something else
**tablet** (TAB-let)—a piece of stone with writing on it

# Read More

**Binns, Tristan Boyer.** *The Statue of Liberty.* Symbols of Freedom. Chicago: Heinemann Library, 2001.

**Heinrichs, Ann.** *The Statue of Liberty.* We the People. Minneapolis: Compass Point Books, 2001.

# Useful Addresses

**American Park Network**
1775 Broadway, Suite 1401
New York, NY 10019

**Statue of Liberty National Monument**
Liberty Island
New York, NY 10004

# Internet Sites

**American Park Network—Statue of Liberty National Monument**
http://www.americanparknetwork.com/parkinfo/sl/index.html
**National Park Service—Statue of Liberty National Monument**
http://www.nps.gov/stli
**Statue of Liberty: Facts, News, and Information**
http://www.endex.com/gf/buildings/liberty/liberty.html

# Index